Rochester Cas

Jeremy Ashbee

CONTENTS

Tour of the Castle

EXTERIOR AND SETTING

The most impressive feature of Rochester Castle is the spectacularly tall keep, which was begun in 1127 by William de Corbeil (c.1070–1136), Archbishop of Canterbury under Henry I (r.1100–35). It stands near the cliffs above the river Medway and is 125ft (37.7m) high, the tallest surviving keep of its period in England, and one of the tallest ever built.

Today three bridges cross the Medway towards London, but from Roman times until the end of the 14th century, when it was replaced by a stone structure nearer the castle, a single bridge spanned the river roughly where the iron road bridge stands today. It carried the main road, Watling Street (now the A2), from Dover through Canterbury to London. The road passed through Rochester as the High Street, only a stone's throw from the castle walls.

These walls follow the line of those that surrounded the medieval castle, which was protected on the three landward sides by a ditch – still visible between the castle and the cathedral. The keep is roughly square in plan, with the projecting forebuilding on its northern side containing the main entrance and chapel. The south-east turret is rounded, unlike

Above: Henry I (r.1100–35), under whose authority the keep of Rochester was built
Below: The two great medieval structures that today still dominate the heart of Rochester, as they did in the 12th century: the cathedral and the castle keep

Facing page: The great keep of Rochester from the east

the other three. The original square turret fell during the siege of King John (r.1199–1216) in 1215 (see pages 28–9) and was rebuilt without an attempt to match the others.

The walls are mostly of irregular rubble stone – 'Kentish ragstone' from quarries near Aylesford and Maidstone – but the angles of the buttresses, doors and windows are yellow Caen stone from Normandy. The rougher stone was covered in lime render in 1240, soon after the White Tower at the Tower of London was similarly rendered. The windows of the lower levels are plain and small, partly for security, but those of the higher tiers are larger and more ornate, as can be seen in the surviving chevron moulding around the arched heads of the highest tier. Just below the battlements on three sides are the lines of holes that held the supports for the wooden *hourds*, or fighting platforms, from which soldiers could drop stones onto attackers below.

Top: The keep of Rochester Castle from the north. A small gate-tower at the turning point on the outer stair once provided additional security at the keep entrance

Above: The White Tower of the Tower of London, shown covered with lime render, as was Rochester keep in the mid 13th century

KEEP
1 Stairway and Entrance

The entrance to the keep was, as now, in the forebuilding, at the top of an external stairway. Such an approach was secure and impressive, placing the entrance at the end of a series of check-points. The two doorways at ground level (one on the outer face of the forebuilding and the other beneath the external stair) were knocked through some time before the mid 18th century. Beyond the second landing in the stair, beside the north-west turret, was a small, two-storeyed gate-tower with double doors controlled by a sentry (see the reconstruction drawing on page 7). The tower was demolished before the 1730s, but traces of the gate arches and vaulted ceilings of the two storeys remain.

The last few steps of the approach bridged a gap in the stone ramp that carries the stairway. They were made of wood, not stone, which allowed them to be broken or removed in case of attack, leaving a gulf nearly 3m wide in front of the entrance doors. The iron canopy above the stair is modern, protecting visitors against grit falling from the walls, but a similar structure was here in medieval times: in 1240 Henry III (r.1216–72) ordered a timber pentice to cover the stairs from the corner gate-tower to the main entrance.

2 Entrance Chamber

The double doors at the head of the stair lead into a large chamber (now the shop). This room was lit by a single-light window beside the doorway, three two-light windows to the north and presumably a further window at the far end (later converted into a doorway). It would have been a light, airy room, but unheated and unsuitable for residence. Instead it served as a waiting room and place in which to transact

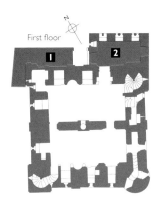

First floor

Below left: The forebuilding entrance in July 1909, before the outer stairway was restored. The remains of the gate-tower can be clearly seen at the corner of the stairway
Below: The single-light window to the left of the entrance
Bottom: The gap between the forebuilding and the solid ramp of the outer stairway was originally bridged by wooden stairs, easily broken or removed in time of attack

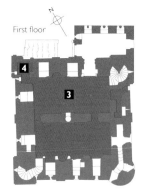

First floor

Above: The doorway from the entrance chamber to the keep

A Cushion capital

B Arch with chevron detail

C Portcullis slot

Below: A bedchamber of the mid 15th century. Rochester's principal rooms led off into smaller, private mural chambers

Below right: View into a latrine chamber in the keep. On the right the square holes of the floor joists can be seen at second-floor level

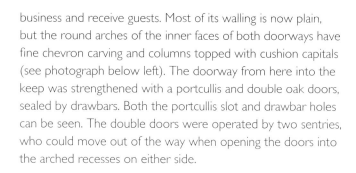

business and receive guests. Most of its walling is now plain, but the round arches of the inner faces of both doorways have fine chevron carving and columns topped with cushion capitals (see photograph below left). The doorway from here into the keep was strengthened with a portcullis and double oak doors, sealed by drawbars. Both the portcullis slot and drawbar holes can be seen. The double doors were operated by two sentries, who could move out of the way when opening the doors into the arched recesses on either side.

3 First Floor

Beyond the forebuilding is the ruined interior of the keep, one of the most impressive sights in English medieval architecture. At some point after the Middle Ages a fire destroyed the interior, with its three wooden floors and roof. Yet without these the magnificent height of the building can be appreciated. The square holes that held the heavy floor joists can be seen in the walls, as can the patches of reddened masonry caused by the intense heat of the fire.

Originally this floor would have been much gloomier, the only light coming from its small windows and from lamps and candles. The size of the windows indicates the need for security at this level, but the rooms are well provided with latrines and fireplaces and were certainly habitable. Perhaps members of the garrison ate and slept here.

4 Mural Chambers

In the north-west turret, and before 1215 almost certainly in the south-east turret, were small chambers. The room at the north-west had a vaulted ceiling and fireplace and led to the upper storey of the gate-tower on the external stair. Although once called 'Gundulf's chamber', after the 11th-century Bishop of Rochester, it was a room for a sentry of the gate-tower.

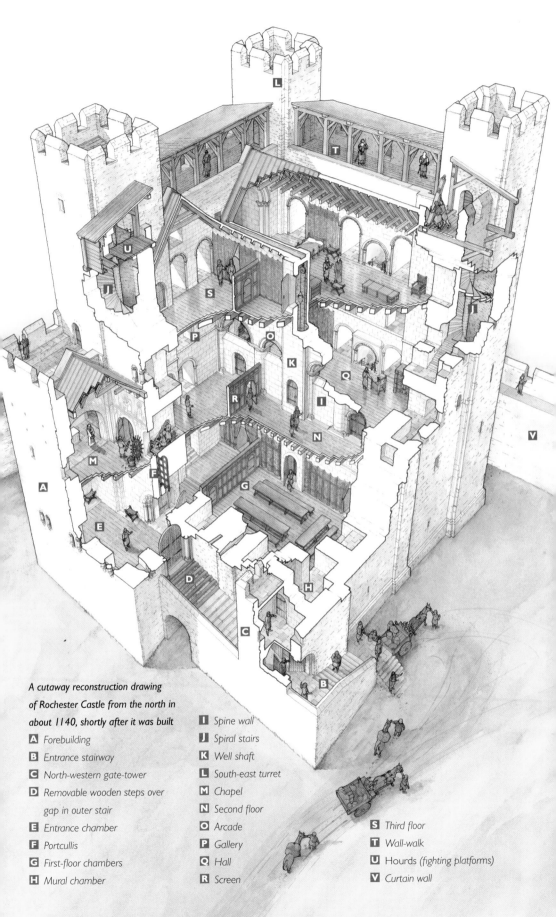

A cutaway reconstruction drawing
of Rochester Castle from the north in
about 1140, shortly after it was built

A Forebuilding

B Entrance stairway

C North-western gate-tower

D Removable wooden steps over
   gap in outer stair

E Entrance chamber

F Portcullis

G First-floor chambers

H Mural chamber

I Spine wall

J Spiral stairs

K Well shaft

L South-east turret

M Chapel

N Second floor

O Arcade

P Gallery

Q Hall

R Screen

S Third floor

T Wall-walk

U Hourds (fighting platforms)

V Curtain wall

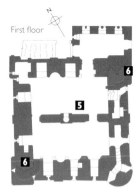

First floor

5 Spine Wall

Opposite the door is a spine wall that runs east to west through the centre of the building, forming a barrier between the two halves of the keep. On the first floor access between the spaces was through two doorways in the spine wall, one at the east end, and one at the west. In 1215, rebels occupying the keep used the spine wall as a line of defence, falling back behind it after King John's men broke through into the far (southern) side.

Below: The massive spine wall has a central well shaft and an arcade at second-floor level. During the siege of 1215 the rebels retreated to the north side of the keep when King John's soldiers broke into the southern side

6 Spiral Stairs

There were spiral stairs in the south-west and north-east corner turrets. The south-west stair began at first-floor level and led to the more important floors above. The north-east stair served all floors, including the basement, and was probably a service stair. Leading off to its right at first-floor

Gundulf, Bishop of Rochester

In his 30 or so years in office Gundulf, Bishop of Rochester (1072–1108), reformed the cathedral community and oversaw various important building projects, of which Rochester Castle was one. He became known for his piety, his kindness to the poor, his loyalty in friendship – and also for his expertise in building.

Gundulf was born in about 1023 in the Vexin, Normandy, and was probably of modest origins. He showed promise as a scholar and studied at Rouen, where he joined the cathedral clergy. In 1057, on return from pilgrimage to the Holy Land, he experienced a severe storm at sea. He vowed to take monastic orders if he survived (which he did), and so joined the Benedictine community at Bec, under its prior, Lanfranc.

William (r.1066–87), Duke of Normandy (later William I of England), appointed both men to his new abbey in Caen in 1063, and after the conquest of England nominated Lanfranc as Archbishop of Canterbury, where Gundulf joined him as head of his household.

In 1076 Lanfranc's new Bishop of Rochester died after only a few months in office, and he appointed Gundulf in his place. The bishopric at that time consisted of a few impoverished canons remaining since the death, some years earlier, of the last Saxon bishop. Within only a few years Gundulf had transformed it into an institution peculiar to

England – a priory attached to a cathedral (by the time he died there were 60 Benedictine monks) – and had rebuilt the cathedral church, of which the crypt and possibly parts of the nave survive.

He quickly gained the reputation of a practical man: in the late 1070s or early 1080s, William I ordered him to oversee the building of his 'great tower of London' (the White Tower that stands today) and in 1088, William's son William II had him rebuild the royal castle at Rochester (see page 26). Substantial remains of

his curtain wall attest to his 'skill and effectiveness in stone-building', as the cathedral's cartulary puts it.

As bishop and frequently suffragan to the Archbishop of Canterbury, Gundulf was prominent in political life: he supported his old friend Anselm, Lanfranc's successor, in his struggles against William II, but he enjoyed the friendship of the next king, Henry I. Gundulf died in March 1108, and was buried in his new cathedral by Anselm.

Left: Gundulf, Bishop of Rochester, as depicted at the entrance to Rochester Cathedral. He holds his bishop's crozier and the White Tower of London, the most famous of his building works

Below: Detail of the opening page of the cartulary of Rochester Priory in the Textus Roffensis, *written in about 1123. It records the grant of land to the bishopric of Rochester*

Top: The north-east spiral stairs. The present entrance to the chapel is visible on the left

Above: *The reconstructed well-head of 1826 at basement level*

Below: *Engraving of the north-east corner of the basement in 1842. The arch on the left leads down to the lower basement; that on the right is the entrance to the spiral stairs*

level is a short stair going up to a secondary entrance, or postern (the draw-bar holes that held the door shut are still visible), with a latrine in the vaulted recess beside it. The postern was reached from outside either by a wooden stair or by a bridge from the east curtain wall. It was presumably built to allow soldiers or servants to enter the building without using the grander entrance through the forebuilding.

7 Basement

The basement, which had no fireplaces, and light and ventilation only from small windows set high in the walls, was built for storage. Its original floor level was roughly that of the present wooden platform, as can be seen from the bases of the doorways. It was only in about 1900, during repairs by the Rochester Corporation, that the floor was lowered to the level of today, when tons of earth were excavated and re-used in a terrace garden on the western side of the castle.

8 Well

The spine wall at basement level has two doorways, similarly placed to those on the first floor. At its centre is the shaft of the keep's well, which rose through and served each floor, but was accessible only from the northern half of the keep. The well-head on this level was rebuilt in 1826 by the then owner of the castle, George Child Villiers (1773–1859), 5th Earl of Jersey, whose crest decorates the stone. The shaft descends 20m into the ground and still contains water.

9 Forebuilding Basements

In the north wall under the wooden steps to the entrance was a window. This was later knocked through to form a doorway. To the right of this doorway are two sets of stairs. One leads to the upper basement (now not accessible) of the forebuilding that was probably used by the cellar-keeper. It had a latrine discharging into the cesspit in the lower basement, which is reached by the next set of stairs.

The other stair leads to the lower basement, which was once imagined to have been a dungeon, but there is no evidence for this. Remains of a wall can be seen that probably formed the retaining wall of the cesspit, while the other half of the pit may have been used for general storage. The doorway in the far wall was knocked through some time before the mid 18th century — originally the only ventilation was provided by the small vent still visible above this outer door.

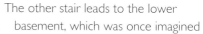

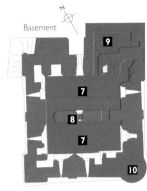

Basement

10 South-east Turret

On the southern side of the basement is evidence of the damage that the keep suffered in the 1215 siege (see pages 28–9). King John's miners dug away the facing stone on the outside of the keep at the south-eastern corner, propping up the overhanging stonework with timbers as they went. They then set fire to the timbers using the lard of '40 pigs too fat to eat', bringing down this entire corner of the keep, including large sections of the east and south walls. The damage was repaired during the reign of John's son, Henry III, but in a simpler style and using a grey–green stone from Reigate, easily distinguished from the original Caen stone.

Above left: The siege of a castle, shown in the 1290 French edition of Vegetius's Art of War. *The besieged drop stones and shoot arrows from the battlements, while the besiegers hurl missiles with siege engines, and approach the walls under cover of mantlets (moveable shelters)*
Below: The semi-circular south-east turret, seen from within the remains of the Drum Tower

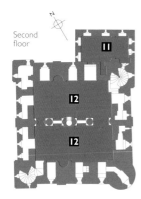

Second floor

Above: The great arch of the original entrance to the chapel from the second (principal) floor

Above right: The chapel, looking towards the apse, where three of its seven windows are visible

Below: Mass in about 1450, as depicted in this French manuscript detail. There were at least two resident chaplains at Rochester Castle

'Seven windows in the chapel will need repairs costing at least 5s., and the carpentry for them will cost 13s. 4d.'
Survey of Rochester
Castle, 1340

🕕 Chapel

The chapel consists of a room divided by a broad, round arch. It forms the top floor of the forebuilding. The present entrance is reached by a short flight of stairs off the north-east spiral stair. It was broken through the back of a niche, probably the sedile, the seat for the priest. The original entrance was the wide door at the west end of the chapel, which gave straight onto the second, principal, floor. It lay, somewhat inconveniently, over the top of the portcullis that guarded the doorway on the floor below: the slot can be seen in the pavement.

The portcullis was operated by a winding apparatus that would have blocked the chapel entrance when in use. It is likely, therefore, that the portcullis was usually held concealed between the two storeys by timber chocks, so that its top rail formed a threshold into the chapel. Only on the rare occasion that the portcullis was needed would the winding mechanism have been brought in to lower it.

Although the position of the chapel is not unusual (other keeps of the time had similarly placed chapels, notably at Orford and Dover), the interior is. It lacks the typical elaborate architectural detail of such spaces, and the chevron decorations and roll mouldings of the keep's other main rooms. Accordingly it was once thought to have had some other function, such as a kitchen, but it is clear from two early 14th-century documents that there was a chapel in the keep and this must have been it. Ornamentation was probably in the form of wall-paintings, lost during the period of at least three centuries when the forebuilding was roofless. Part of the original stone vault that formed an apse over the altar survives over the eastern room. The central door leads to a cupboard, probably a vestry. The roof over the western nave was installed in 1986, slightly higher than the original timber roof.

🄲 Second (Principal) Floor

The second floor is one of the most impressive spaces in a castle in England, and contained the grandest rooms in the keep. It includes a mezzanine level to give the rooms extra height, and the spine wall is pierced to form an arcade of four round-headed arches. Today the archways are open, but antiquarian drawings and traces in the stonework show that a masonry wall was added between the columns. A fragment remains in the westernmost bay, its doorway with chevron decoration identical to that on the main arcade, showing that it was added very soon afterwards. Above this partition wall the spaces below the arches were left open, and light, sounds and smells would have passed between the two chambers.

The height and layout of this floor, and the architectural detail of its arches, windows and fireplaces – richer than that on any of the lower floors – speak of its grand function. The round columns, 'scallop' capitals and round arches with chevron ornament call to mind the nave of nearby Rochester Cathedral, which was remodelled after a fire in 1137, exactly when the keep was being built. The detailing of the keep is simpler than that of the cathedral, but between them the two buildings display the sophistication of Norman architecture in Kent in the second quarter of the 12th century.

Above: An engraving of 1830, looking towards the arcade. Remains of the walls that originally blocked the arcade up to the level of its 'scallop' capitals still existed at this date

Below: The arcade today. Within the arch on the right remains part of a doorway that once led through the arcade wall

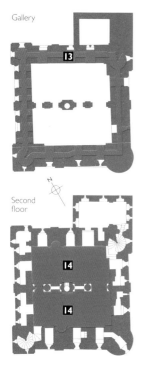

Gallery

Second floor

Above right: The gallery on the west side of the keep, overlooking the principal floor

Below: The remains of an arch on the third floor in the south-east wall of the keep, with a smaller replacement window set into it. This corner of the keep was rebuilt after the 1215 siege

13 Gallery

A gallery built into the outside walls ran around the entire upper section of the second floor, through all four corner turrets. Arches allowed extra light into the rooms from the windows in the outer walls and fine views into both principal chambers. On the east side the gallery passageway rises six steps, then falls three. Around the corner to the south it falls a further six steps. This corner of the tower was rebuilt after its collapse during the 1215 siege (the crack in the wall and vault of the passageway where the rebuilt stonework meets the original is visible). The change in level was not part of the rebuilding: it reflects a feature of the building's original design, an arch that is now missing.

The Missing Arch

From the inner-facing windows of the south gallery the southern half of the east wall can be seen. At the top (the third floor) are the remains of a tall, rounded arch. The rest of the arch and the walls below it collapsed in 1215, and it was replaced with a smaller window. A similar arch is thought to have existed on the floor below, its apex at about the height of the nearest arch in the spine wall arcade (which is slightly taller and wider than the other three). To accommodate the high arch on the principal floor, the gallery rose and fell again over its apex. This arch would have formed a niche, probably with a window looking out to the exterior.

Such niches are thought to have been the settings for thrones, tables or other important or fixed items of furniture: other examples can be seen at Chepstow in Gwent, Castle Rising in Norfolk and the White Tower in the Tower of London. At Rochester it was probably the high table, at which the lord and his closest intimates dined, that stood under this arch, and possibly the builders gave an additional 'frame' to the high table by building a further arch, spanning the easternmost bay of the room.

◱ The Hall

The principal floor probably functioned as a hall divided into two rooms, north and south. The spiral stairway (see page 8) in the north-east turret would have been the service stair, leading to all floors, including the basement, and opening onto to the northern room of the principal floor.

This northern room functioned partly as a thoroughfare, giving access to the chapel and to the well (workable only on the north side of the spine wall on each floor), and to a latrine in the east wall. It was the more public and lower in status of the two rooms. Only by passing through a door in the spine wall (probably one at either end, as on the floors below) could the more privileged visitor enter the inner (southern) room, where the most important guests might dine with the lord.

The Archbishop of Canterbury oversaw for the king the building of the keep in 1127, and it has been suggested that the keep had accommodation for him, as well as for the king. This could explain the division of the hall into two, or the addition

Below: A richly decorated fireplace on the southern side of the keep. It would once have warmed the hall, where the king and his household dined

Bottom: *When at Rochester, the king would have dined in splendour with his household, as does the king in this French manuscript illustration of about 1445*

Battlements

Third floor

of a floor above the principal floor – a unique arrangement, as such an addition is not seen in any other keep of the period. But it is difficult to imagine two such magnificent households – those of the king and the archbishop – occupying the building at the same time without causing chaos. It is more likely that the archbishop simply managed the castle in the king's name, and was expected to stay there only rarely. It would have been the king, rather than the archbishop, who held court in the hall of the keep.

15 Third Floor

The north-east stair continues to the third floor. There is a good view of this floor from the battlements at the top of the stairs. As on the lower storeys, this floor consisted of two large rooms, one on either side of the spine wall, and a number of smaller spaces in the thickness of the external wall, many of them embrasures for windows. Though lacking the height of the second floor, these rooms had equally fine ornament, with decorative mouldings to windows and fireplaces. The presence of fireplaces suggests the rooms were designed to be inhabited, although, unlike on the second floor, there are no fixed latrines, which suggests an occupant of high status who instead had the use of a close-stool.

If the rooms below were the king's hall, these would have been his chambers, where he, his family and closest courtiers lived, slept and kept their most precious possessions. In the east wall of the southern room remains one side of the tall rounded arch (see pages 14–15) that would have served as a niche for a throne or a table, or even a bed. Its presence reflects the fact that a 12th-century monarch had little privacy: day and night, he was to some extent on show.

Above: Looking into the corner of the north-east tower at third-floor level
A Medieval pigeon nesting boxes
B Traces of the steep pitch of the 12th-century roof
C Holes for the third-floor joists

Right: A king conducts the business of state from his bedchamber with courtiers and officials in this French manuscript illustration of 1409. Similarly, when at Rochester, the king would have led a life of little privacy, even when in his private apartments on the third floor

16 Battlements

The battlemented parapet around the top of the keep is mostly original 12th-century stonework. On each side it has five merlons (raised sections of the crenellations) between the corner turrets. The wall-walk beneath it was rebuilt at the end of the 19th century by the antiquary and architect George Payne (1848–1920) at roughly the level of the medieval walkway. Originally there would have been a low protective parapet around its inner edge. Payne found evidence of timber beams that had run through the outer parapet and extended outward. Some of the holes can still be seen for these beams, which formed fixed supports for the wooden fighting platforms, or *hourds*, put up as required. The 13th-century seal of Rochester shows similar beams projecting from two of the keep turrets. On the east, north and west sides of the keep were doorways, now blocked, allowing soldiers to climb out onto the platforms.

The view into the interior of the ruined keep is impressive. On the inward facing walls are traces of the medieval roofs: in the northern half, the steep pitches of the 12th-century roofs with drain outlets to either side, and in the southern, the shallower lead-covered roof put in during the repair work after the 1215 siege. On the north side, above the level of the roof, are a number of small holes in the keep wall. These are medieval nesting boxes for pigeons, restored in the 1890s.

Above: Rochester keep from the east. The door, now partly blocked, that gave access from the battlements to the fighting platforms on this side is immediately above the central buttress

Below: Armoured soldiers defend a keep from its battlements in this illustration made in south-east England, possibly Rochester, between 1325 and 1350

Medieval Castle Life at Rochester

For much of the Middle Ages, the castle bailey at Rochester was dotted with buildings and the scene of much activity – only occasionally warlike.

At the heart of the castle community was the constable, usually a knight, who commanded the garrison of soldiers and crossbowmen, originally for the Archbishop of Canterbury, and then, from the 13th century, for the king. The constable and his household of family and servants usually lived in the castle, probably occupying the keep, or perhaps the royal apartments when the court was absent.

During peacetime the garrison of a castle such as Rochester was not large: about 30 men would have been normal. But 30 armed men had to be fed, clothed and altogether provided for and so service buildings of various sorts occupied the bailey, together with those who worked in and about them.

There would have been craftsmen such as smiths, carpenters and stone-masons, together with their workshops: 14th-century inventories list stores of stone and timber and various tools used in the castle. There were also several stables, one of which, built in 1248, was 80ft long and 16ft wide (nearly 25m long and 5m wide), manned by a number of grooms. Similarly the kitchens, buttery, and servery had their staff, and there were at least two resident chaplains, serving the chapel in the keep and the two chapels in the bailey.

The castle's period of greatest prosperity was in the mid 13th century, when Henry III and his queen, Eleanor of Provence, regularly stayed in their hall and chambers in the bailey (see page 31). But several of these buildings were badly damaged during the siege of 1264 and not rebuilt. Through the theft of materials, the damage caused by storms, and simple deterioration over time, the number of buildings diminished. By the 1380s the bailey contained little besides workshops, and the inhabitants lived in the towers on the curtain wall or in the keep.

Top and bottom: Craftsmen fashion weapons in a forge (top), and servants transport royal possessions while others roast birds on a spit (below), in these details from a Flemish manuscript of about 1340. Such work would have been a feature of daily life at Rochester in medieval times

Above: *An English sword dating from 1250, of the sort that would have been made, sharpened, and on occasion used, at Rochester Castle in the 13th century*

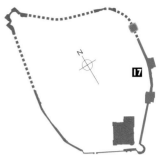

17 EASTERN CURTAIN WALLS

The current castle entrance to the north-east of the bailey lies near the site of the medieval main gatehouse, the last of which was demolished in 1871. Originally there was a broad ditch outside the walls, across which a drawbridge connected the gatehouse to a stone causeway that ran close to the line of the present road. Parts of the causeway remained until 1888.

The two rectangular towers in the eastern walls were built for Edward III (r.1327–77) in the 1360s. That closest to the keep replaced one of the 12th or 13th century. Between the towers four arches (visible from outside the castle) form the foundation of the wall: the medieval ground level was about a metre higher than today. The opening between the towers is modern.

In the 19th century the ditch was used as a cemetery: many gravestones remain against the wall. Charles Dickens, who lived about three miles from Rochester for the last 13 years of his life, reputedly wished to be buried here. A row of houses stood in the southern part of the ditch until the early 20th century.

Above left: Rochester Castle in the 1860s, showing the ditch outside the east curtain walls cluttered with houses and gravestones
Below: The eastern curtain walls today, with the two towers of Edward III and the broad ditch. Against the low wall to the right are stacked 19th-century gravestones

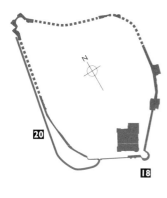

18 DRUM TOWER

The drum tower stands at what had been shown to be a weak point in the castle's defences: the area undermined in the siege of 1215. It was added during the repair work of the 1220s by Henry III, allowing soldiers to overlook the road from the south. Today two tiers of crossbow loops remain, but an engraving of the 1670s shows a third tier above them, and originally the tower would have been topped by battlements, providing a fourth tier of shooting positions. Inside it would have had timber floors, but remained open to the rear.

From further towards the river is a good view of the semi-circular south-east turret, which replaced the turret destroyed in the siege. Beside it can be seen the great fissure down the south side of the keep, which shows the line of the collapse in 1215.

19 BOLEY HILL

To the south of the castle is the area called Boley Hill, a medieval name probably referring to birch trees planted there. Once believed to be the site of an early motte-and-bailey castle, or even a Viking camp, Boley Hill is now recognized as an outer enclosure of the medieval castle. It was reached by a drawbridge across the ditch, the remains of which are under the present road, and protected by banks and ditches (parts of which survive in the garden of Satis House, the private 18th-century house facing the castle). This outer enclosure contained a number of stone buildings: a medieval cellar of one of these survives under one of the houses on the hill.

Below: Illustration of Rochester Castle from the south by William Stukeley in 1722. The drum tower is in the foreground. A drawbridge once crossed the deep ditch on the left, connecting a gatehouse at the south end of the bailey to Boley Hill

20 RIVERSIDE

The footpath around the side of the castle leads to the Esplanade beside the river. In the 19th and 20th centuries the chalk cliff was reinforced with stone several times. The rough stonework above this modern facing is part of the base of the

Roman city wall; above this is the distinctive herringbone stonework of what remains of Bishop Gundulf's wall of about 1089. The crenellations were added in the 18th century, but to the north, before the gap, the upper parts date to the 13th century and are the remains of Henry III's chamber block: two blocked windows are clearly visible (see pages 22–3).

Beyond the chamber block are early 20th-century arches built using rubble taken from the basement of the keep (see page 10) to support a terrace. The medieval wall that stood here may have been destroyed when Elizabeth I (r.1553–1603) allowed stone to be taken for the building of nearby Upnor Castle.

The ragged stonework at the north-west corner was part of the bastion built by Richard II (r.1377–99) between 1377 and 1384 to overlook a new stone bridge across the Medway. Traces remain of two spiral stairs that led to an upper storey, as well as a shaft running down to the waterside: it was possibly used to raise supplies to the bailey from the river, or formed the chute of a latrine with a door to allow access to clean it out. Now only the lowest parts of this bastion survive, but a view of 1735 shows these ruins in a more extensive state (see pages 22–3). The present stairs and arch in the Norman style were built in 1872 to give access to the new public gardens. The vaulted medieval basement of the tower was destroyed to make way for the stairs.

Top: The drum tower, with the semi-circular south-east turret of the keep beyond it

Above: The Victorian doorway in the Norman style that was knocked through the remains of Richard II's north-west bastion in 1872

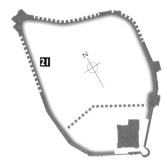

21 BAILEY

In the mid 13th century the bailey would have been filled with buildings, people and animals (see page 18). On the west side was the king's chamber block overlooking the river (two of its windows, now blocked, remain). It was built during Henry III's works begun in the 1220s, and it was here he stayed on his frequent visits to Rochester.

In the early 20th century George Payne (see pages 17 and 40) cleared the western wall of ivy and restored its medieval features, such as the windows of the chamber block and, below them, the joist holes for the upper-floor joists. Below the joist holes are the arches of the understorey, probably a storeroom. The upper chamber adjoined a chapel: in the 1250s

Below: Rochester Castle Gardens in about 1910. Queen Victoria's Jubilee memorial of 1887 is on the left

Left: The 1735 engraving of Rochester Castle from the river by Samuel and Nathaniel Buck; it shows how close the 14th-century bridge was to the castle, leading directly past the remains of Richard II's north-west bastion. The doorway at the base of the bastion can be seen at the level of the river bank

Below: Remains of the king's chamber block, built by Henry III in the 1220s, with its blocked windows and the arches of its understorey. Henry's chapel was later built to adjoin it

Henry III complained twice about 'strangers' passing through his chamber to the chapel. Further south are four embrasures, once open over the river, but now blocked.

A cross-wall with a gatehouse once divided the bailey into two. The line of this wall is lost, but on the east side of the bailey the tower nearest the keep bears a scar where it met the curtain wall. Some of the principal bailey buildings were burnt in the siege of 1264 and not rebuilt. Between the 15th and the 19th centuries the bailey was divided into small plots, some used as gardens by tenants. These were cleared when Lord Jersey (then the owner of the castle) and the city corporation turned the bailey into public gardens, which opened as the Castle Gardens in 1872, as they remain today.

History of the Castle

ROCHESTER BEFORE THE CASTLE

From the first century AD a bridge existed over the Medway at what was to become the city of Rochester. Here the river cut across the main Roman road from Dover and the coast to London. It was almost certainly the Roman army that built the bridge as well as various staging-posts, inns and stables for officials and wayfarers using the road. By the early third century the Roman settlement of Durobrivae (from the Celtic, meaning 'the fort by the bridges') had a stone wall enclosing about 23 acres (9.5ha). Part of this wall survives on the cliff above the river where it was incorporated in medieval times into the defences of the castle.

With the end of Roman rule in Britain in the early fifth century, Rochester's fortunes declined, until two centuries later, in 604, when King Ethelbert of Kent established Rochester as a bishopric and founded a cathedral dedicated to St Andrew. The remains of this small building are marked out under the west front of the present cathedral, which was begun in about 1082. In the ninth century the Roman walls were still strong enough to afford protection from Viking attacks; but when the Norman conquerors swept across England, they needed more powerful fortifications to mark and defend the land they had taken.

Above: A Roman glass bottle, found under Rochester Bridge. By the early third century the Romans had settled at Rochester, which was then called Durobrivae, 'the fort by the bridges'
Below: Odo, half-brother of William the Conqueror, urges on the Norman soldiers at the Battle of Hastings while brandishing a club, in this detail of the Bayeux Tapestry. As a bishop, Odo was forbidden to carry a sword, but this did not prevent him trying to hold Rochester Castle against the new king, William Rufus, in 1088

THE FIRST NORMAN CASTLE

It was almost certainly William I (r.1066–87) who built the first castle at Rochester, after his conquest of 1066, to protect the crossing at this point on the river Medway. Domesday Book describes the castle in 1086 standing in the south-western corner of the walled city, on land owned by the Bishop of Rochester. The Normans raised the ground by several metres when building the castle and remains of pre-Conquest Rochester may well survive beneath the Castle Gardens; but it is likely that this part of the late Anglo-Saxon city was sparsely populated when the castle was built.

The first castle was largely a structure of timber and earthworks, and almost certainly on the site of the present castle, rather than on Boley Hill to the south-west, as was once claimed. The Roman walls in this part of the city seem to have been pulled down to create the castle defences: their foundations were buried under an earth bank that was then topped with a timber palisade.

BISHOP ODO AND THE FIRST SIEGE

At his death William I divided his lands between his elder son, Robert, and his younger, William II ('William Rufus', r.1087–1100), giving England to William. In June and July 1088, the castle saw action during a violent conflict between William II and his rebellious uncle, Bishop Odo of Bayeux, who supported Robert. Odo, during the reign of his half-brother William I, had been for some time the most powerful man in the land after the king, and had been made Earl of Kent, one of

'Odo now carried off booty of every kind to Rochester, plundering the king's [William II's] revenues in Kent, and especially the lands of the archbishop, breathing eternal hatred against him, because, he said, it was by his advice, that his brother had cast him into chains'.
William of Malmesbury (c.1090–1142)

Above: William Rufus, as depicted on a coin of the time. William defeated his brother Robert and his uncle Odo to retain the Crown of England

Above: Funeral of William the Conqueror in Caen (left), and (right) the crowning of his son William Rufus by Bishop Lanfranc, in a Netherlandish manuscript of the 1460s. William Rufus's brother, Robert, and their uncle Odo challenged his claim to the English Crown, leading to the first siege of Rochester

Below: Remains of Gundulf's crenellated 11th-century curtain wall, on the western edge of the bailey

his chief residences being at Rochester. In the dispute between the Conqueror's sons, Odo's forces took control of the city and castle. In the heat of the summer, the king built two wooden 'siege castles' and blockaded the city.

After several weeks, weakened by sickness and plagued with flies, Odo's garrison surrendered, and Odo was banished abroad, where he joined Robert. He died in 1097 on the First Crusade.

BISHOP GUNDULF'S STONE CASTLE

During the siege the castle probably suffered damage, as did the nearby cathedral, and William II saw the need to strengthen it. Within weeks of the siege he commissioned the Bishop of Rochester, Gundulf (d.1108), to rebuild the castle walls in stone (see page 9). In return for this work William renewed the grant of the manor of Haddenham in Buckinghamshire to the monks of Rochester, without the fee of £100 he had previously demanded. Gundulf agreed, thinking the work would only cost him £40: in fact it cost £66 (but as the manor was worth £40 per year, this was a favourable settlement for the monks).

A decade earlier, Gundulf had supervised the construction of the 'great tower of London', now the Tower of London's White Tower, for William's father. At the time of the commission to rebuild Rochester Castle he was building a new cathedral church in the town. Understandably the cartulary (monastic records) described him as 'very experienced and efficient in building in stone'; a substantial length of his well-built stone wall with distinctive herringbone masonry can

Left: Builders at work cutting and lifting stone and sawing wood, in a detail of a French manuscript of about 1400. The 'noble' and 'outstanding' Rochester keep, built more than 250 years earlier, took about ten years to complete
Below: The complicated status of Rochester Castle – a royal stronghold entrusted to the archbishops of Canterbury – meant it was frequently a source of friction between the king and the archbishop, as it was between Henry II and Thomas Becket. In this detail of an English manuscript of 1307–27, the king and Becket are depicted arguing

still be seen overlooking the river. Although obscured by later heightening, this section of the wall includes a rare survival: the original 11th-century crenellations.

THE BUILDING OF THE KEEP

The most significant development of Rochester Castle was a collaboration (as was the construction of the stone wall) between the Crown and Church. In 1127, Henry I (r.1100–35), who had succeeded his brother William II in 1100, entrusted the custody of the castle in perpetuity to the archbishops of Canterbury. Again, the king imposed a condition: that the then archbishop, William de Corbeil (d.1136), was to build a fortification within the castle walls. The resultant tower – the present keep – was probably almost complete when de Corbeil died in November 1136. It was described at the time by chroniclers as 'noble' and 'outstanding', quite justifiably: it remains remarkable for its slenderness and height, and is thought to have been the tallest building of its type in Europe.

Though the Crown had entrusted the castle to the archbishops of Canterbury, it remained a royal stronghold through the 12th century. Henry II (r.1154–89), grandson of Henry I, spent over £150 on it during his reign, part of it when the archbishopric was vacant. The castle was on occasion a source of friction between the king and the archbishop, as during the period in which Henry II's relationship with Thomas Becket (d.1170) was deteriorating. But the most serious conflict came during the reign of King John (r.1199–1216), the last surviving son of Henry II, and would escalate into one of the most famous castle sieges in English history.

'For he [Langton] is a notorious and barefaced traitor to us, since he did not render up our castle of Rochester to us in our so great need. And also because, though frequently requested and repeatedly summoned, he has not done us the service he was bound to …'
King John, writing in 1215 to Hubert de Burgh about Archbishop Langton

Above: *Detail of the tomb effigy of King John at Worcester Cathedral*
Below: *Seal of Robert Fitzwalter (d.1235), one of the leaders of the rebel barons and one of the 25 signatories of Magna Carta. In October 1215 Fitzwalter briefly held the bridge at Rochester against King John*

FIRST BARONS' WAR AND SIEGE OF 1215
King John and Archbishop Langton
From 1211 Stephen Langton was Archbishop of Canterbury. King John had persistently blocked Langton's election since 1206, causing the pope in 1208 to place England under an interdict (suspension of ecclesiastical functions and privileges) and, the following year, to excommunicate the king. So, John was forced to accept Langton as archbishop, and made an agreement with him that the castle would be placed for fixed periods in the hands of his own men, and when it was in the hands of the archbishop he requested it to be held 'in such a way that by it no ill or harm shall come to us or our kingdom'. In the summer of 1215, however, shortly after the barons had forced John to agree to Magna Carta, this arrangement, which had never been honoured by Langton, collapsed, and the king's enemies assumed control of the castle.

The Rebel Barons
The strategic importance of Rochester and its river crossing was crucial: the rebels needed to hold the castle to protect London (then in rebel hands) from the king, who had been raising an army in Kent. The rebels duly installed a garrison at the castle under William d'Aubigny. On 12 October, Robert Fitzwalter (d.1235), one of the 25 signatories of Magna Carta and a leader of the barons, attempted to hold the bridge at Rochester against the king's assaults. But the royal army seized and broke the bridge, forcing Fitzwalter to retreat to London. They then laid siege to the castle, having cut off its garrison from reinforcements. Fitzwalter had pledged to return with support, and did later in the month, but his relief expedition of 700 did not reach Rochester. Hearing at Dartford of the large forces John had managed to muster while yet maintaining his siege force, he turned back to London.

Contemporary letters give more detail about the destruction of the original south-east turret of the keep, into which the defenders retreated. On 25 November John commanded Hubert de Burgh, his justiciar (chief political and judicial officer), to work day and night to send him with all speed '40 pigs, too fat for eating, to raise a fire under the tower, so that our business there may take no longer'. Miners had dug away at the stone wall and placed timber props under the overhanging masonry. Using the pig fat they now fired the props and brought down the corner turret, and large parts of the east and south walls on either side.

The King's Victory
Even this catastrophe did not immediately end the siege. The rebels, retreating to the northern half of the keep behind the spine wall, were able to hold it for several days more. They had nothing but water to drink and horseflesh to

'The king was pressing the siege with full force and allowing them no respite, bombarding them ceaselessly day and night with five stone-throwing engines … Then miners were sent in. One side of the building was brought down, but the defenders took up a strong position in the other half, for the keep was built in such a way that a very thick wall separated this part from the side which had fallen. Never in our age has a siege been driven so hard, or resisted so bravely.'
John's siege at Rochester, as told by the 13th-century Barnwell chronicler

eat, 'which was particularly hard on them, having been brought up in luxury', and finally starvation forced them to surrender. Reportedly John was dissuaded from hanging every rebel baron by one of his captains, who reminded him of the dangerous precedent this would set: 'Lord king, we have not yet won the war. I beg you to consider what different turns a war can take. If you make us hang these men, the barons fighting against us will not hesitate to hang me or your other nobles when they get the chance. Do not let this happen – not a single man in your service will fight for you on those terms.' It seems that John listened, and only one man was hanged: a crossbowman whom allegedly the king had fostered from childhood.

This was a significant victory for the king. As the Barnwell chronicler concluded, 'some rebels fled in fear back to London, others took refuge in monasteries, and now there were few who cared to put their trust in castles'. But the king's triumph was short-lived. The following year the rebels regained the castle and only in 1217 was it securely in the power of the new king, John's son Henry III (r.1216–72).

Top: The gutting of a pig shown in an English manuscript of about 1300. King John ordered '40 pigs too fat for eating' to be sent to him at Rochester, where their fat was used to fire the props holding up the undermined south-eastern tower

Above left: *Soldiers undermine a tower beneath the cover of a mantlet in this French manuscript detail of about 1325. From the battlements the besieged rain down on them missiles and burning torches as the rebels would have done on the king's men at Rochester*

Below: Henry III, as shown in a detail of an English manuscript of the 14th century. Henry came to the throne at the age of nine in 1216, the year after the siege of Rochester Castle. He went on to make many additions and repairs to the castle

THE WORKS OF KING HENRY III
Repair of the Keep

The castle in 1217 was in a sorry state, and the regents of the child king were faced with an urgent need to repair it. The most urgent, or most achievable, works were those to the curtain walls. Only from 1226 is there evidence for repairs to the keep, half of which stood as a roofless ruin. The stonework repairs were well advanced by 1232, when oaks were needed for new flooring.

The repairs are easy to see in the keep today: grey-green Reigate stone was used instead of the original golden Caen stone, and although the builders copied the Normans' round arches, the mouldings are plainer. The new wooden floors were supported on an internal timber frame, rather than on joists set directly into the stonework, and the roof over the southern half of the keep was much flatter than the Norman one. But the most obvious change was that the new south-east turret was circular, not square. Similarly the tower in the south-east corner of the curtain wall, rebuilt presumably at this time, was round. While the design follows the contemporary fashion for round towers, it may well have been in part an attempt to avoid vulnerable corners that could be undermined.

The Bailey Buildings

Henry III visited Rochester at least once a year most of the years of his long reign, on his way to and from Dover and the shrine at Canterbury, and gave frequent instructions to his officials to correct deficiencies he found in the castle's buildings. These instructions provide many details about the buildings that once stood in the bailey, which included a large, rectangular great hall with stained-glass windows, as well as kitchens, a buttery, a servery, two chapels and a two-storey building for the king's wardrobe (where his possessions were stored). There would also have been stables, forges and workshops.

In 1239 the king ordered that the chapel be whitewashed and decorated with a wall-painting of Christ, and in 1244 an additional chapel was built next to the king's new chambers (see pages 22–3). The surviving fragment of a building overlooking the river, with two blocked windows and the arches of a once vaulted lower floor, is probably the remains of this new chamber block built for Henry in 1221. Writs also describe repairs to the main gate in 1248 and 1259, to a postern gate on the south side, leading to an outer bailey on Boley Hill, in 1225 and 1226, and to the building of a cross-wall, dividing the bailey into two parts, in 1231 (see page 23).

Above: Rochester Castle from across the Medway. The remains of Richard II's north-west bastion are on the left, and further south, to the right, are those of Henry III's chamber block overlooking the river

Below: Of the many building in the medieval bailey, one was the king's wardrobe, where his possessions were stored. In this manuscript detail of about 1340 men carry an iron-bound storage chest

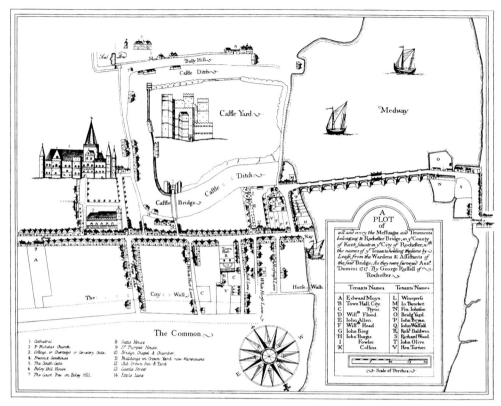

Rochester: the Crown and the Church

Top: A map of Rochester as surveyed in 1717 by George Russell of Rochester. Note the gatehouse and causeway at the north-east of the bailey, and the drawbridge at the centre of the 14th-century bridge

Above: Rochester Cathedral from the battlements of the castle keep

Rochester has never been a large city, but throughout its history, powerful institutions have jostled for prominence and space inside its walls.

Those walls, built by the Romans in the late second or early third century AD, defined an area of only about 23 acres (9.5ha): tiny compared with Canterbury at the time, which was about 130 acres, or London which was about 330.

For a thousand years, the city hardly expanded outside this boundary. But if the later medieval copies of charters of the seventh century are to be relied upon, about half the area within the city walls (an area largely abandoned after the collapse of Roman rule) became the property of the

Church. From 604 a cathedral was established here. Early bishops of Rochester included such eminent churchmen as the Roman missionary Paulinus (d.644) and Ithamar (d. before 664), who was the first native-born bishop in England.

It was on land granted by the Church that the first castle was built soon after the Norman Conquest of 1066. Domesday Book records that this castle, established by William I, stood at the south-west corner of the city, an area once belonging to the Bishop of Rochester. In exchange for this land the bishop received the royal manor of Aylesford. By the 13th century an outer bailey was added to the castle, outside the

Left: The remains of Rochester Priory cloister in 1805, by John Buckler
Below: Coin minted at Rochester between 1205 and 1207, under King John, who is depicted on its obverse crowned and holding a sceptre

city's southern boundary. This area is now known as Boley Hill.

South-east of the castle the cathedral priory expanded through much of the Middle Ages. In the 1340s, the monks were given permission to build a new city wall south of the old defences, enlarging the priory's outer court, where the bakehouse, brewhouse, granary and barns stood.

South-west of the cathedral (the present College Green), facing both the cathedral and castle, was the palace of the bishops of Rochester, built in the 11th or 12th century.

Traces of the medieval palace remain in the present buildings there. The whole complex of priory and bishop's palace was surrounded by a stone wall in the 1340s, forming an enclave within the city.

Rochester High Street preserves the line of the Roman Watling Street, always the mercantile heart of the city. Although the buildings lining this street are mostly of the 18th and 19th centuries, the long, narrow plans of the properties reflect the boundaries of their medieval predecessors. Outside the city

is another reminder of the ancient origins of Rochester: the road bridge. Built in the 19th century after the destruction of the medieval bridge that lay slightly further west, it crosses the Medway where the old Roman bridge used to carry Watling Street on towards London.

Below Rochester from across the Medway, 1799, by Edward Dayes. The medieval bridge still stands

Above: A crossbowman and an archer aiming their bolt and arrow, in an English manuscript detail of about 1400. Crossbowmen and archers played a major part in both 13th-century sieges of Rochester

Below: The rebel barons rode their horses into Rochester Cathedral, and used it as their headquarters for the siege of the castle. They reputedly treated it and its inhabitants brutally. In this Netherlandish manuscript of the 1470s a knight rides into a sanctuary with his sword raised

SECOND BARONS' WAR AND SIEGE OF 1264

Henry III's authority was challenged by his barons, as his father's had been, leading in 1264 to the third siege of Rochester. The leader of the rebel barons was Simon de Montfort (d.1264), Earl of Leicester. He aimed to capture Rochester from its royalist garrison, under the command of Roger de Leybourne, and various noblemen, to safeguard the rebel hold over London and prevent a royalist resurgence in Kent.

Montfort attacked from across the river, while his ally Gilbert de Clare, Earl of Gloucester, led another assault from the east. On Good Friday, 18 April, Montfort crossed the river (burning ships to create a smoke screen and perhaps to damage the bridge) and attacked the castle, using the cathedral and priory as his headquarters. The next day he broke into the bailey to find that the garrison had burned down the king's hall to deny it to the attackers and had retreated into the keep. On Easter Sunday, both sides observed a truce, but Montfort resumed his attack on Monday, using siege engines to bombard the tower, and sent in men with picks to undermine the walls.

The defenders were close to surrender when, on Saturday 26 April, Montfort took fright at reports that Londoners were about to defect to the king, and lifted the siege. Less than three weeks later, Montfort's army defeated the king at Lewes, Sussex, and the rebels finally took control of the castle.

Damage and Repair

Although the damage done in 1264 was less than that in 1215, this siege had graver consequences for the castle. Henry III regained control of his kingdom in 1265, and had some of the damaged buildings repaired, such as the great gatehouse at the north-east corner. But the residential buildings in the bailey were never rebuilt. A certain John Potyn, an official at the castle, took the opportunity to pilfer lead, timbers, roof-tiles and stones from the decaying buildings, and in 1281, Henry's son Edward I (r.1272–1307) ordered that the hall and chambers, 'long since burnt', should be pulled down and their

Horses in the Cathedral

'Earl Simon set fire to the bridge and the wonderful defences on it, and after making many attacks and employing many ruses, he forced his way into the city … Gilbert de Clare fought his way through from the other direction with a huge army and, as was usual, they looted the whole city and everything in it. Most horrible of all, his devil soldiers entered the church of St Andrew with swords drawn … They laid violent hands on the gold and silver and other treasures and carried them off … Armed knights rode around the altars on horseback and with sinful hands dragged away those who took refuge there … all the holy places were used to stable the horses, the whole place was filled with the dung of animals and the filth of dead bodies.'
Account by the monks of Rochester, early 14th century

Queen Elizabeth Bruce at Rochester

Shortly after her coronation in 1306, Elizabeth, wife of the Scottish king Robert Bruce (r.1306–29) was captured by a Scottish baron sympathetic to the English and sent to England. She was held in a succession of houses, nunneries and castles in poor conditions, until in March 1314 Edward II had her moved from the Tower of London to Rochester: he instructed the constable to assign her a chamber fitting one of her rank, allow 20 shillings a week for her expenses, and to let her take exercise under escort in the bailey and walk across to the cathedral 'at suitable times'.

While Elizabeth was at Rochester, her husband defeated Edward II (r.1307–27) at Bannockburn in June 1314; she was now a valuable means to ransom captured English nobles. In July she was sent back to the Tower of London and, with her sister-in-law, exchanged for the Earl of Hereford. She reigned as Queen of Scots until her death in 1327.

materials reused elsewhere. Unusually for a royal castle, the old keep, rather than buildings in the bailey, became the main residential building for the rest of the Middle Ages.

A CENTURY OF DECLINE

As the 14th century progressed, the castle steadily declined. Many references to it are concerned not with royal residence but with the custody of prisoners, such as Elizabeth, wife of Robert Bruce of Scotland, held here in spring 1314.

By the 1340s, most of its buildings were in serious disrepair, including the keep, whose stonework, timber and lead were all in need of renewal. In the 1360s surveyors twice reported that little had been done, and that the situation had been made worse by successive constables and their officers, who had removed more materials. In March 1363, the castle was badly damaged in the great storms that struck the south of England. By 1369 the only buildings reported left standing were the keep, the 'first and second gates', and a hall, kitchen and stable.

Above: Elizabeth de Burgh, wife of Robert Bruce, depicted in an English armorial of the 16th century

Below: Engraving by Samuel and Nathaniel Buck of 1735, showing the now destroyed main gatehouse, repaired by Edward III in 1367. Between the gatehouse and the drum tower to the far left are Edward's two mural towers, built at the same time as the gatehouse

Above: Richard II depicted on the opening page of a letter written to him in France in 1395, at the same time as the building of his new bridge at Rochester

Below: An armed party attacks the Archbishop of Canterbury and the king's ministers during the Peasants' Revolt of 1381 in this detail from a late 15th-century edition of the Chronicles of Jean Froissart

Unsurprisingly, Edward III (r.1327–77) showed no inclination to stay at Rochester, and in any case, he had other residences nearby, including a manor at Gravesend and a new castle underway at Queenborough on the Isle of Sheppey. Only in 1367 were repairs begun at Rochester. An account from the time lists a bell ordered from London to ring the working hours for the builders. The repairs included works to the main gate and the rebuilding of much of the east curtain wall, with the enlargement of an old tower and the building of a new one (the two rectangular towers visible today, see page 18).

KING RICHARD II

Four years into the reign of the young Richard II (1377–99), Rochester saw two disasters in a single year. In early February 1381 Rochester bridge collapsed. It had been kept in repair since it was built by the Romans in the first century AD, but when large blocks of ice that had formed in the hard winter broke loose in the sudden thaw and smashed into the stone piers, it was finally destroyed.

In the summer of the same year, the castle was attacked and taken for the last time. The aggressive pursuit of taxes by Richard II's officials was the final straw in a series of grievances against the king. Uprisings began in Essex in May. On 9 June, Trinity Sunday, a party under the leadership of Robert Baker of Dartford broke into the castle and released a prisoner, Robert Bellyng, and then marched on through Maidstone and Canterbury to London. But by the end of the month the revolt had been put down and most of the leaders executed.

The works begun in 1367 at Rochester by the king's grandfather, Edward III, now continued. A large new tower, begun in 1378, was completed in 1383 at the north-west

The Peasants' Revolt

'They went to Rochester and sent their people to the villages about. And on their way they beat down and robbed houses of advocates and procurers of the king's court and of the archbishop, and had mercy on none … They went to the castle and took the knight that had the rule of it … The knight, seeing these people in fury and ready to slay him, feared death and obeyed them, and so they took him with them against his will'.
Account of the peasant uprising by Jean Froissart, c.1388

corner of the bailey, facing downstream towards a possible line of attack by French ships. This bastion would have given extra security to the old bridge, but the new stone bridge – begun in 1382 a year after the collapse of the old one – was built even closer to the castle, and so better protected by the new bastion. Although this bridge has also now gone, its position is marked by the Bridge Chapel, which was also begun in 1382, at the southern end of the new bridge. The bridge took about ten years to build, and in 1395–6, it received additional security with a drawbridge and a winding-house, for the machinery to raise and lower the bridge, midway across its length.

Above: The 'new' bridge begun in 1382 under Richard II, after the old Roman bridge finally collapsed. This photograph of 1856 shows the bridge the year before it was demolished: the broad arch at its centre had replaced the original medieval drawbridge
Below: Sir Anthony Weldon, by an unknown artist. In 1610 James I granted Rochester Castle and its income to Weldon

THE TUDORS AND STUARTS

Almost nothing is known of the castle in the 15th century. In the 1440s there is a reference to 'farmers and tenants' renting parts of the bailey for use as orchards and gardens, and during the remainder of that century and the next, the outer bailey on Boley Hill and parts of the castle ditch on the eastern side were similarly divided up and let to tenants. The strategic value of Rochester was declining.

In 1559 and again in 1600, Elizabeth I licensed the removal of stone and brick from the castle walls to build and extend a new artillery fort at Upnor, opposite the naval dockyard at Chatham. Despite its ruinous state the castle still had an income from castle guard rent, which dated back at least to 1201. This rent was owed by local estates that had had a share in the duty to maintain the defensive strength of the castle. In 1610, James I (r.1603–25) acknowledged that the old castle had no military value, but granted it and its income to a courtier, Sir Anthony Weldon (c.1583–1648).

During the Civil War the Weldon family supported Parliament and the castle seems to have escaped the 'slighting' (deliberate damage to make a castle indefensible) that ruined many Royalist strongholds. Nevertheless, by the mid 1660s, the keep had lost its roof and floors. Reddening of the stonework inside the keep shows that there was a violent fire, though it is

Pepys at Rochester

'Thence to Rochester, walked to the Crowne, and while dinner was getting ready, I did there walk to visit the old Castle ruines, which hath been a noble place, and there going up I did upon the stairs overtake three pretty mayds or women and took them up with me, and I did 'baiser sur mouches et toucher leur mains' [kiss their mouths and touch their hands]

and necks to my great pleasure: but, Lord! to see what a dreadfull thing it is to look down the precipices, for it did fright me mightily, and hinder me of much pleasure which I would have made to myself in the company of these three, if it had not been for that. The place hath been very noble and great and strong in former ages.'
Samuel Pepys, writing in his diary on 2 October 1665

Above: Samuel Pepys painted by John Hayls in 1666, just a year after his encounter with three young women on the stairs of Rochester Castle

not known when or how it broke out (see page 6). When the artist Francis Place drew the castle in about 1670, he showed it with decaying battlements and large cracks and clumps of vegetation in the stonework. Still more evocative is a series of entries in the diary of Samuel Pepys, who visited Rochester on several occasions in the 1660s when on naval business at Chatham – once in the company of 'three pretty mayds'.

THE CASTLE IN RUIN

During the 18th and 19th centuries Rochester Castle continued to decay. The only inhabitable buildings were the two rectangular towers of the east wall, to which timber-framed cottages and outbuildings had been added. The other towers,

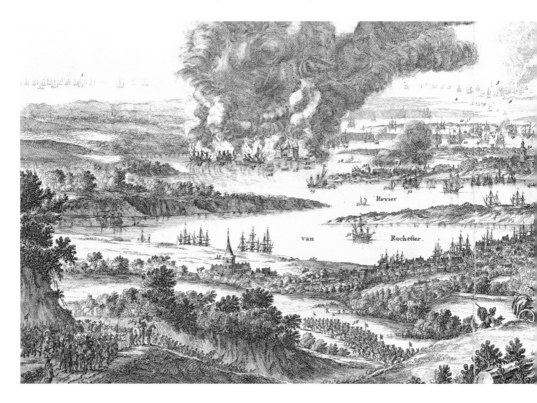

chamber block and gatehouse stood in ruins and trees were growing throughout the bailey. In the mid 18th century, the castle housed Spanish prisoners of war.

Weldon's descendants sold the castle in the 1730s to Thomas Blechynden, after whose death in 1740 it was sold to Samuel Child (d.1752), an eminent banker. In 1780 the commander of the Royal Engineers at Chatham sought permission from the Child family to convert the ruins into an army barracks, but the plans came to nothing. The last of the Child family to own the castle was Victor Child Villiers (1845–1915), 7th Earl of Jersey, whose grandfather had carried out repairs to the keep in 1826, including the refitting of the well shaft and head, on which his crest is carved (see page 10).

Above: Rochester Castle in about 1670 by Francis Place. The projection on the far left of the ruined curtain wall is the remains of the gatehouse that once gave access to the drawbridge leading to Boley Hill

Left: The Dutch fleet burning English ships on the Medway near Rochester in 1667, during the second Anglo-Dutch war, print made in 1687 after a painting by Willem Schellinks

'There was Rochester castle … standing in the solemn shadow of its walls, looking up at the blue sky, its only remaining roof (to the disturbance of the crows and jackdaws who garrison the venerable fortress now), [I] calculated how much wall of that thickness I, or any other mere man, could build in his whole life'.
Charles Dickens, *Household Words*, 6 September 1851

Above: *Charles Dickens reading to his daughters Mary and Kate in the garden of Gad's Hill Place, near Rochester, in 1865*
Below: *Rochester Castle today*

THE CORPORATION OF ROCHESTER

In 1870 the earl's estate leased the castle to the Corporation of Rochester, which in 1884 bought the freehold, and opened the castle grounds to the public as a park and tourist attraction.

Photographs of the Castle Gardens at this time show broad gravel walks between lawns, herbaceous borders and flower beds, and the keep partly covered in ivy. The creation of the public gardens led to the destruction of some historic features. In 1872 the last remains of the castle's main gatehouse were removed. In the same year steps from the Esplanade above the river to the Castle Gardens were built through the remains of Richard II's tower of the 1370s, and the builders removed most of the vaulted chamber of the tower's undercroft.

On the north side of the castle a new road and houses encroached on the bailey and destroyed traces of the curtain walls. Yet, despite much loss, there were some significant discoveries, for example in 1888, when parts of the medieval bridge that had led to the main gatehouse were found.

ROCHESTER IN RECENT TIMES

From 1896 to 1904 several buildings in the castle were repaired under the supervision of George Payne (see page 17) and the City Surveyor. They concentrated on the keep, consolidating the mural galleries, wall tops, battlements and corner turrets, and excavating the basement to the present level. The main concern was the cliff above the Esplanade, which needed support. It was revetted in stone in 1931, extending the revetment of 1872. In 1965 the responsibility for the keep was assumed by the Ministry of Works, and so passed in 1984 to English Heritage, where it remains today. Since 1995 both the keep and the Castle Gardens have been managed by the City of Rochester, now Medway Council.